JUST IS

Olive Vussere

Order this book online at www.trafford.com/07-0443
or email orders@trafford.com

Most Trafford titles are also available at major online book retailers.

Note for Librarians: A cataloguing record for this book is available from Library and Archives Canada at www.collectionscanada.ca/amicus/index-e.html

ISBN: 978-1-4251-2039-9

We at Trafford believe that it is the responsibility of us all, as both individuals and corporations, to make choices that are environmentally and socially sound. You, in turn, are supporting this responsible conduct each time you purchase a Trafford book, or make use of our publishing services. To find out how you are helping, please visit www.trafford.com/responsiblepublishing.html

Our mission is to efficiently provide the world's finest, most comprehensive book publishing service, enabling every author to experience success. To find out how to publish your book, your way, and have it available worldwide, visit us online at www.trafford.com/10510

www.trafford.com

North America & international
toll-free: 1 888 232 4444 (USA & Canada)
phone: 250 383 6864 • fax: 250 383 6804
email: info@trafford.com

The United Kingdom & Europe
phone: +44 (0)1865 722 113 • local rate: 0845 230 9601
facsimile: +44 (0)1865 722 868 • email: info.uk@trafford.com

10 9 8 7 6 5 4 3

"What we are looking for is what is looking."

St. Francis of Assisi

Preface

What started this was a series of questions about intuition, gut feelings – that kind of knowing and guidance that does not depend on reason. Though the entire progression along this thread of thought has not been included here, this account begins with an attempt to take a fresh look at the Bible, as if it had never been heard of before – a big challenge in itself, considering a background of being raised with it. As you will see, it didn't take long to come to a radically different view of the implications. What is found right at the beginning casts a new light on all that follows.

Quantum theory and various philosophies seem to give a comprehensive response to these questions with comparative ease. However, the intention has been to follow this line of inquiry through to see where it takes us, allowing all possibilities – even the possibility that truth is everywhere.

It has been my privilege to compile communications from these fictionalized anonymous characters. Your happy indulgence is hoped for with regard to this desire for anonymity; any reaction at all is currently felt to be a distraction from a total surrender of outcomes. And besides, it's from *all* of us here.

If you please, be intrigued.

Olive Vussere

In company with Myone A. Muse

and

U. Ardt-Reamin

p.s.

Please note: The following may be nothing but an expression of perceptions and opinions, which is presented by an individual who has insubstantial regard for such. As always, be your own guru.

Correspondences from

Myone A. Muse

And

U. Ardt-Reamin

Chapter One

Forbidden Fruit

Hello U.

As you know, I have been attempting to read the Bible like I never heard of it before. I hope you'll find this interesting enough to respond to.

Was the forbidden fruit (of the tree of the knowledge of good and evil) in the Garden of Eden really nothing but a test of obedience? That's one explanation I've heard, but I wonder if it could also have been a warning about something. The term "knowledge of good and evil" sounds to me like another way to say "knowing right from wrong". As you can see, I didn't get very far before coming to a major belief shaker. I've always thought we are *supposed* to know right from wrong, or at least try to. But if knowledge of good and evil (to "know right from wrong"?) was intended for humanity, why was it forbidden?

First I'd like to understand better just what this knowledge of good and evil is. One other apparently well accepted definition is something like this: 'The fruit of the tree of knowledge of good and evil refers to the power to decide for oneself what the standard of good and evil is, a claim to complete moral independence'. If I'm understanding correctly, this theory suggests that to make up our own standard with accountability to no one else is what is forbidden. Implied, is that what is especially forbidden is to claim non-culpability in relation to God; and that does sound reasonable. I can accept that we are accountable to our source, at the very least in so far as optimum functioning is concerned. So then is it: Do not eat of the tree of I-don't-need-God? (Well, then I wonder how to look at Gen. 3:22 NIV: "The man has now become like one of us, knowing good from evil." Did that "us", knowing good from evil, have an attitude of I-don't-need-God? And, were they divided, did they adhere to separate standards?)

I do have a problem with that definition; it doesn't quite add up. And it just brings us right around again to knowing about good and evil; the interpretation that the forbidden fruit is a reminder that we are accountable, implies that we can know what is good and what is not, and that we need to know - or else! To me that sounds exactly backwards to the actual instructions, which are more like: you don't need to know and you better not try to, or else. ("You are free to eat from any tree in the garden; but you must not eat from the tree of the knowledge of good and evil, for when you eat of it you will surely die." Gen. 2: 16, 17 NIV) And the part about accountability seems a bit redundant to me; the need to be in accord with God (accountable) is a given, it's too obvious to need a threatening reminder. (On second thought, it may not be so obvious if one thinks of God as being limited within a personality.)

I find it noteworthy that Eve took the fruit because she believed it was, among other things, "desirable for gaining wisdom" (Gen 3:6). I've often heard that it was because she wanted to be morally independent of God (which is how and why she was deceived presumably); but I guess that was actually just speculation. And when they gained enough knowledge to realize they were indecently exposed, they hid from God. (Gen 3:10) "I was afraid because I was naked; so I hid," Adam says. They hid because of their shame and fear, not because they intended to separate from God. They obviously *felt* separated, but I don't read into it that that had been their plan. Apparently one does not require a mutinous attitude in order to taste the forbidden fruit.

If I just read it like I've never heard about it before, it's all backwards to normal. The normal way of looking at it seems to contort itself around to a perspective from which it can ignore the fact that gaining the knowledge of good and evil was clearly advised against (Gen 2:17). So rather than ignore the apparent details and get ahead of myself wondering how to know who's interpretations are right, I'll back up a bit and try some other perspectives.

Is it just the ability (or intent) to know the difference between good and evil that we're talking about here? Is that what the forbidden fruit is - the intent to know the difference? Is it just what it sounds like; is it simply the knowledge of what is good and what is evil that Adam and Eve were told not to take?

And, was it even actually "forbidden"? Sounds to me like it could just be information, and not necessarily with any threats or promises attached, just clear instructions and information: "... but you must not eat of the tree of the knowledge of good and evil, for when you eat of it you will surely die." (Gen 2:17 NIV) In other words - it's not good for you. They apparently didn't die that very day, except maybe compared to what they had been up till then, or maybe they *started* to die that day. Maybe aging and disease wasn't a sure thing until they ate the fruit. It could be that drawing conclusions (about what's good or evil, for example) draws conclusions to us. Conclusions stop something. Death is a conclusion. Anyway, I'm not sold on the idea that God forbid this knowledge as a test, or because of a need to be reassured of mankind's obedience or fear of punishment.

So, if we look to the Bible for knowledge of what God deems good behaviour, why ignore the first instructions?

A question from another perspective: Could the forbidden fruit be nothing other than knowledge that there *is* a difference - are we not supposed to believe that good and evil exist? End of discussion, if that's the case. But I don't think we need to hurry out and try to find some way to convince ourselves that we believe there's no difference between good and evil, that good is no different than not good. Beside the fact that I'm going with the idea that the Bible has merit here, I'd say there is a difference, there is such knowledge. And obviously, the specific instructions given to Adam and Eve would have drawn their attention to the difference if they weren't already aware of it.

So (unless 'you must not eat of the fruit from the tree of the knowledge of good and evil' actually means 'go get the knowledge of good and evil because it'll be on the test for your final grade') then it must be the *difference* we're not to know; the "forbidden fruit" is knowing the difference between good and evil. (Or *trying* to know…) Just what it sounds like - the knowledge of.

That seems radically backwards! As I said, I've always thought we're *supposed* to know the difference - right from wrong. Wow! Can that logic be right? I'm finding it difficult to accept. What do you think about it? I'm going to try it on; if nothing else it will unveil a few fears.

Yes, it is definitely backwards to what I've always believed, but it does help me with Gen 3:22 (NRSV this time): "… man has become as one of us, to know good and evil." Apparently God knows the difference (and whoever the "us" is), and that knowledge is not for mankind. Once Adam and Eve partook of that knowledge, it seems they were no longer compatible with the garden God had put them in. Looking at it that way, there is a difference but it's God's business not ours (and besides, it's not good for us).

The Bible starts with the story of how it came to be necessary, how we got in trouble in the first place; and the rest of it seems to be about how to deal with all the trouble we continually get into from voluntarily (and unwittingly) meddling in God's business. We might say, the Bible is God providing us with tools, better ways to deal with the things we now "know" to be shameful. As in the Genesis account: at first (Gen 2:25) they felt no shame, and then after the fruit (3:7 and: 10) they wanted to cover their nakedness, and then (3:21) God gives them tools (clothes) to more adequately deal with the discomfort of their chosen way.

God also prevents them from remaining forever in this state by removing access to the tree of life. Although, if Adam and Eve really were after the particular knowledge that would make it *unnecessary for them to hear God,* then they probably also would assume that God was jealous of his tree of life and didn't want to share with the competition. How unsettling, to think of the ultimate order of things as being that petty and insecure. Or maybe the God of the Bible is not GOD - not the ultimate order of things - but merely a god? Personally, if I read it innocently, without fear or pretense, I take God to be

GOD, both personal and impersonal.

Here's one other theory before I send this over to your court: the forbidden fruit was created to allow for free-will so a person could voluntarily and consciously choose to trust God, rather than only because there was nothing else to choose. Humans have the capacity to be sentient beings with their wits about them.

Interesting Subject

I could say, "Yeah you're right, I agree that the implication is that we really actually are not meant to judge", but we can't leave it at that, can we. We are addicted to the forbidden fruit by now, and we need another fix. We absolutely must know what God's standard is, right? And what isn't. We insist on owning the knowledge of what is and what isn't. Proof; we want proof of the truth. We even think we are justified in our need for it.

God basically says right at the beginning, "Go play and don't worry yourself with my business. Trust me; I've got a handle on it." But I guess we need another fix so let's take another bite.

You take it from here; you're the one always stuck on knowing.

Needing to Know

If this (needing to know) is biting the forbidden fruit again … well, I don't know about that. Is that what you were implying? I am sure though, that I want to be living according to God's standard, and besides, **any other standard can't be anything but a pretense.** Whether you're talking morals and religion, or just about how it works and you have some other more scientific term for God, like the energy field or something - "God's standard" *is* "how it works"(not necessarily the same as how we think it *should* work). So who's going to tell me what the true standard is?

A lot of people sincerely believe they can tell you what the Truth is. They have the facts and the proof. All these different people surely don't tell you the same thing though, and they often use the same facts and references as proof against each other. So, how can we know who's right? I wonder if it's even *possible* to figure out who's right. Can we know?

Sure, we can *believe*; we can cling to the belief that "it's true, so naturally we believe it." *But a thing doesn't have to be true to be believed.* Wars, and even our daily lives, illustrate this constantly.

Most people I know who believe in God say he/she is good, is love, merciful, etc.; but many say, "God is either not all-powerful, or is good *and* evil and can't be trusted." And it would appear so … yup, especially if you ***know the difference*** between good and evil. Hmmm …

One of the most horrible, potentially damaging things that ever happened to me turned out to be the very thing through which the most wonderfully life changing insight came about. So do we still call that evil, when it turned out to be good?

I'm back to that question again: "Can we know?" If we can, the next question is, "who's right and who's wrong?" Maybe you're right; as far as I can see, we *are* still looking for the knowledge of Good and Evil, only with nicer, more refined names maybe. I have to wonder why. Why are we not content with the knowledge of Just Is? Why do we need reassurance about this? Is it so that we can know we're right, and therefore **okay for the future**? Is knowing we're right part of God's intention? Big question, that.

Maybe God wants something more intimate and fresh, something that's new every moment. Maybe we *can't* know, in order to prevent us from being stuck in the dullness of certainty. Maybe we're made to function best moment to moment rather than concerning ourselves so much with the future. It is our enthralled involvement with the future which causes us to seek reassurances about all its unknowns, is it not? We as a culture certainly have a fixation with psychological security, to the point that a lack of it seems to be an excuse for almost any sort of behaviour, so long as striving for it is taking up most of our energy.

So here I am, with at least some fairly clear ideas of what I think of as being good or as being evil. Then I read the Bible (and watch the news) and have to conclude that: (1) I have no idea after all; or, (2) God is good *and* evil; or (3) God is just not all-powerful. Or maybe I would just try to blow it off by concluding that the Bible is not a true word of God anyway, but only contains some truths, mostly in the New Testament and definitely not in Deuteronomy 13 for example (instructions on stoning and putting to the sword anyone who entices you to worship other gods, and also all the people who live in their town and all the livestock too - hopefully never meant to be taken literally).

But like I said, I want to see where this goes if I follow it through on the assumption that the Bible is God's word, even though the possibility exists that it may only be partial and poorly translated.

On the other hand, whether I give the Bible credit or not, I seem to be left with these conclusions: God is good *and* evil, (at least according to the standard

I go by) and/or God is not everything and everywhere, not all-powerful).

The trouble with these conclusions is that **I am judging God**!

Now when I say God, I'm thinking in terms of GOD, all the word implies: all-powerful, all-knowing, all-present, The All in All, the Source of everything. Obviously, the only relevant standard is that of the source and origin of all that is, *so how could I think that God is either wrong or a wimp just because I don't agree?*

God is not GOD because I would do things differently?! Ludicrous!

That leaves me with the fact that I really don't know what is good and what is evil. As much as I would like to, I cannot seem to find any intelligent conclusions about this. "I don't know" doesn't seem like much of a conclusion. I find this all rather unsettling. The urgency (which I am suddenly aware of) to draw some kind of conclusion, is in itself alarming. You're right, I am stuck on knowing.

So eventually we might say, "Okay God, you be GOD; knowing good from evil is your business and I accept whatever you do as good and right". But we're still left wondering how to know what God would consider to be good and right behaviour on *our* part - how to know what behaviour "works", what is in accord with the true standard.

I know many people would answer that by saying, "We have the answers. It's God's standard we believe in, it's all there in the Bible". But as I've said, everyone reads it differently. And what about other Bibles claiming to be God's word? Or newly discovered ancient manuscripts? Or modern ones, psychically channelled? We're back again to judging who's really on God's side – who's right and who's wrong about the truth. Basically we're back to trying to *know the difference* between good and evil, once again.

Maybe E V I L is just to L I V E backwards to the original intent. (I wonder if others who have said something like that were looking at it this way.)

Chapter Two

Suspending Belief

Moment

There is a moment of great moment – a point at which one meets a belief. I don't mean only an idea which has been proven or reasoned out to be true; it might be a belief so basic it may never have occurred to you as being something to question, or even as being a belief at all. In this moment of meeting, of recognizing a belief as a belief, one considers its value and origin.

Now, if you feel the resistance to this questioning, but stay with it rather than escape it, you have managed something quite momentous. (It can be very difficult in the sense that it requires attention and the utmost alertness.) The conflict is often uncomfortable and at times painful and terrifying. Since most of us have a basic belief that pain is to be avoided at all costs, and a lot of practice at doing just that, it becomes easy to "justify" falling into one of the endless escapes readily available.

You are the one. (This has relevancy to your last missive) You are the only one who can tell you what your fears are, and if you have been successful in facing them. You are the one who can teach you freedom.

Whoa! Let me guess the escapes you're using in resisting those statements.

~ I can't be the one, I don't know enough
~ There are others more wise, learned, evolved… who must guide me.
~ That's just my ego saying I'm the one.
~ We need to work at it first, in time maybe I can be the one.
~ We need some one to make sure we're not fooling ourselves.

(Let me know how close I came.)

The reasons and justifications (which are all based on beliefs, you'll notice) are endless. But the question is: why do we have the resistance to letting go of a belief in the first place? Even just the idea of *suspending* that belief for a moment to see what it's like without it, sets up a huge resistance sometimes. ("Sentient beings with their wits about them," to be sure.)

Do we think we can't go back to it once we leave it? Or is it a feeling that we are betraying a trust somehow? (Who would require such mindless loyalty?) Or maybe we unconsciously believe it won't be true anymore if we let up on believing in it. Do we think our belief makes it true? And keeps it true? Do we know something we don't know we know?

I can hear you say, "No! If it's true, then it's true – whether I believe it or not." Well then, why do you feel such resistance to the possibility of having your beliefs made unbelievable, if it'll be true anyway? That's silly, isn't it? I suspect you're afraid of offending the ones who have brought you to the belief, helped you see the light. St Paul maybe, or Jesus (since you're using a Christian point of view). Or maybe it's some flesh and blood "guru" – preacher, teacher, friend, scientist, artist, author…? Ultimately, I suspect it's God you're afraid to offend. Why would that be? Possibly because of a belief in a place of eternal punishment? Maybe the way you read it was, "Believe in hell and thou shalt be saved". Do you really think God is so small as to be offended if you wonder if someone is putting words in their mouth? (He, She, It, They, Us… God is All.)

But I digress. Though maybe not as far as you might at first think. Some may worry about the biblical hell, to others a social blunder is hell. I think what we're talking about is the idea of judgement and consequences.

Back to the question of resistance to having our

beliefs made unbelievable. For some reason we find ourselves defending the beliefs and conclusions we identify with, even the ones that make us miserable. For example: I used to believe I was unhappy in my marriage. I defended that belief with all the reasons why I was unhappy till it was obvious there was no way I *could* be happy. It seemed entirely unreasonable, even horrifying in a way, to consider suspending that belief, because I *knew* it was the truth. "So why pretend otherwise", I said. "Why deceive myself? I'm quite right to be unhappy – see, I have all these good reasons."

And that may have been more intelligent than blindly smearing something pretty over it like perfume over a stink, and calling it positive thinking. I'm not suggesting denial here, but rather, awareness: just plain paying attention and noticing how hard you cling to your familiar patterns.

Eventually I asked myself, "If you could be happy, would you? Or are you refusing to be happy until you get whatever it is that will *make* you happy?" I realized that I was choosing to be miserable for a good reason, rather than to be happy for no reason.

It is never having the desired thing, that makes you happy. Happiness is in not struggling. (I don't mean effort, that's different than struggle as I mean it here; there is often much happiness in effort.) You might think getting what you wanted caused your happiness, but really it was quitting the struggle that allowed it; when you get the desired thing, you let go of the resistance to the idea of not having it, for a moment. Aahhh … happiness. But if that attachment is still there, the struggle will soon return in the form of resistance to losing what you gained, whether it be food for the hungry, a new yacht, or respect from your peers – it doesn't matter at all what it is. Happiness is in dropping something, letting go, rather than in picking something up. (If you're still into the Bible, I could quote something about a camel and the eye of a needle here, but I guess that would just be my interpretation of it so never mind.)

This is how I look at it: If I am not happy, there must be something restraining me as tightly as I cling to it. I know, that's a lot like someone telling you to let go of the lifeline in order to live. That is often how it feels.

Anyway, as you know, the marriage ended in spite of all my happiness, but do you see that that is beside the point? The point being that I could be happy without any justifications or reassurances. I suspended the belief that a reason or explanation is required, and just let it in uncensored. I can go back to being miserable anytime I want to, if I miss that identity too much. And I don't even need a marriage for that.

It would appear that this too, is backwards to what we've thought: We're not limited to having emotions about what is. What is, however, is limited by what we emote. (Limited is probably the wrong word. Created, might be better.) Our emotions are not created by what is; what is, however, is created by what we emote.

We don't have to feel a certain way just because of what is happening; circumstances do not choose our emotions – we do.

ꟷ

```
Re: Moment
  Suspending belief? Expand on that
please.
```

ꟷ

Suspending Belief:

It's not original with me, I borrowed the phrase. I can only tell you what I personally mean by it: To suspend a belief does not mean to replace it with something else. Get this – I do not mean, to turn belief into disbelief, or should into shouldn't, or any variation thereof. I just mean to allow the possibility that you don't know for sure, one way or the other.

If you try this sometime, be ready to watch your mind. You as much as anyone I know of, are sold on the idea of KNOWING. You're adventurous; I even hear you are fearless. HA! Try the unknown. I mean the *unknown* – as in the unknowable. You are familiar with the unknown of new lands and jobs and people, and making them into the known. That's not what I'm talking about.

As I was saying, watch the "yes buts" from your mind. "Yes, but I have proof! And reasons – good reasons!" You can still suspend it, proof or not. If you really look at it, and your perceptions tell you that indeed the rock is falling, go ahead and move out of the way. Like I said, don't try to change belief into disbelief, or disbelief into belief. (You would be just as flattened either way.) Just allow the possibility that you don't know for sure.

The point of all this, is that if you are going to choose a belief to stick with as the ultimate and unchanging truth, you base it on knowledge. (Stop for a minute here and think about knowledge: when you *really* know something, there is no doubt, no question, no need of proof or labelling, no need of threats and promises – all of which are usually only given to compensate for some doubt or uncertainty. But we haven't come to that kind of knowing in this discussion yet. It's different than just having a justifiable belief, or becoming convinced.) Here's my point: partial knowledge only gives us perceptions and opinion. It's like knowing math but not rabbits and being confused to find that 2 and 2 can make a lot more than 4. And besides, things change without notice.

Knowledge, to be of any value in finding absolute truth, must be absolute itself. Who has that kind of knowledge? Only GOD, I'm thinking. Science and religion certainly don't. Look at all the back-pedaling they both have done throughout history.

Spare me the "yes buts". Maybe all it needs is a little more information and that "yes but" will change too; proof disproves proof all the time. How do you know? You don't. You can believe you know. But why do you need to know anyway? As you've said yourself, it's about the future; when ever you feel upset about not knowing, it's because you are seeking some kind of psychological security, reassurance about what something means for the future. You don't need to justify a desire for security to me; I'm just saying it's a false security if it's based on knowledge. Unless of course, it's an absolute and total knowledge.

If you can be okay with the insecurity of not knowing, you will be in security; then you will be trusting the All of everything. You'll be trusting instead of acquiring knowledge, trusting God – that is, GOD – rather than trusting knowledge which is obviously limited. So my comment is: Don't be so insecure in your relationship with the All in All.

Hmmm...

So then I ask myself: "Do I want to trust or do I want to know?" Well certainly I want to know. No blind faith for me. **Is it either trusting knowledge or trusting God?** Maybe it can be both, but I suppose one will carry more weight than the other when it comes right down to it.

We've seen how knowledge must be total and complete to be of ultimate value. What about trust in God (the Source, Life, Great Spirit ... what ever word you like today)? What do we know about trusting God completely? What would that even look like? Have we ever seen that? How could we know that's what we saw, or didn't see? Could we prove it? Obviously not. I don't think that kind of knowledge can go there.

Something I notice is that knowledge looks for God somewhere "out" there. Trust looks inward for God. Trying to find ultimate truth about God through knowledge of proof, must come from a belief that God is separate from us. Whereas trust must spring from a belief that God really is the *All* in All, and the kingdom of God really is "within you".

Proof - results of scientific experiments for example - as much as the intuitive insights we get, are all part of GOD. The questions I have are about the interpretation of any of this information. Ultimately, does proof interpret and approve intuition, or does intuition approve proof?

Yeah, I want to know, but I'm also beginning to see that I can't know enough to be truly secure. It makes sense to trust the All in All, and if you asked me I'd say that I do, even though I still look for reassurances that it's smart to do so. But if I think about it, seeking psychological security (knowledge as proof I'm right) about God (including what God wants of me) is like me asking you for your watch to hold till you get back with my camera. I don't completely trust you; I need reassurance. You're right again - I am insecure in my relationship with the All in All.

I think a question I could ask myself is: Am I trusting God, or waiting until I *know* I can? (How much knowing would that take, anyway?)

Another Question

What is conscience? It seems to be a sort of inborn standard of conduct, and if so, it's an ingredient in the human recipe - God given. Our conditioning (the beliefs and patterns one acquires) will shape a conscience or influence it, though I doubt if it could totally replace it. But I wonder, if you could take the conditioning away, would one be compatible with all other unconditioned consciences? Whether it is innate or learned is a good question. I suppose I'm back to conclusions and the security of *knowing* again - in this case, whether conscience is or is not God given - before I dare consider trusting it as the template of God's standard. I'm still trusting acquired knowledge before God.

What about intuition? What's to keep God

from communicating with us personally from the inside of us? I guess it doesn't matter what word you use - intuition, conscience, still small voice, Holy Spirit… we even know someone who calls it a cricket. What ever you call it, how do we know that's not the voice of God? Is this not guidance and direction in response to signals from our bodies or the world around us?

Bystanders

The preferred belief, however, seems to be that we're innocent bystanders, victims of evil. Well, isn't that what we're saying when we maintain that we're born sinners, or naturally faulty for whatever reason? "*Don't give me the responsibility of hearing God, I can't be trusted.*" It seems much easier to be helpless victims (maybe blame our parents, or Adam and Eve …) than to consider any possibility that might require our attention and response ability – we're playing it safe.

Playing It Safe

Yes, it does seem safer to follow the laws and guidelines (proven facts or accepted behaviour) than to directly follow God. Is that partly because, if the guidelines are wrong we're off the hook? We seem to believe that being fooled is a way of being excused. (And it's somehow far more excusable to be fooled by someone else than to be fooled by our selves.) So we give our power away, becoming helpless as a way to ensure that we will be blameless; we think playing *victim* (though we might try to gloss it over with other names like loyalty or selflessness, duty or devotion, and say it's for the greater good) is the *safest* route. And that of course, is not too intelligent since we're volunteering for the *certain* pain of being a victim now, in the hopes of avoiding pain in our future that is *not certain* - the *potential* pain of our *possible* mistakes! And why do we want to avoid making mistakes? Isn't it basically to ensure our safety and comfort - isn't it that we want control of things so as to avoid pain of some kind? A big part of that pain we avoid, does seem to be the pain of blame. The lure of martyrdom - insane.

This reminds me of the subject of selfishness. What is bad about being selfish? It seems we don't want the responsibility of thinking for ourselves about as much as we don't want the responsibility of looking after ourselves, so we look for an escape. Selfishness seems to be generally accepted as an entirely rotten thing to be, which provides a very respectable escape, or avoidance. "What is bad about selfishness" seems like a stupid question, I know - but is it?

If selfishness is bad, then its opposite must be good, right? And that would be: to consider the needs and wishes of others to be more important than my own. (As escapes go, respectable *and* convenient.) But is it really so bad to take care of yourself first, so somebody else doesn't have to try to do it - someone who can only guess at what you really feel or need? (While you guess at what they need?)

Selfishness

If selfishness is not good, does that mean we should stop it? Why, because it's bad for others? God wants us to? If we quit it because we fear judgment then that's more selfish (self preservation) than altruistic, I think we can agree. But even if we quit it for some fearless reason, like just because it pleases God and others, it's still self oriented because that's what our self desires – to please God and others. It is our privilege, something we do because we like it, want it, choose it. It's something we do for our selves, like forgiveness is, or going fishing.

I am not advocating taking care of your own interests at the expense of others, which by the way, I think is a learned response rather than a natural born tendency. But the very intention to be unself-ish is self-ish, because it is what we desire to be as a personal preference, for whatever reason. It is also self-ish because it is obviously not in our own best interest (true to ourselves) to wilfully hurt others. We reap what we sow; what goes around comes around; do unto others … (and if we don't understand how that all works we'll probably get an opportunity to learn more about it).

Golden Rule

Doing something that's true to yourself is ultimately for the Love of God, for All that Is, since we are all one. It's kind of like refusing to be co-dependent. A person who is not afraid to be labelled selfish would naturally refuse to be a co-dependent, or an "enabler", to someone with a destructive habit. They wouldn't need an expert to tell them how it works, they would do it naturally by being true to them-selves. Remember, the Golden Rule is *not,* "Do unto others as they would have you do unto them." It's,

"… as you would have others do unto you."

If you're just plain true to yourself (self-ish) then you don't need to have knowledge of what's good or bad for someone else before you apply tough love, or before you treat them as you would like to be treated. If you're true to yourself it happens naturally, with or without approval. Love is not limited to having "a prove all" from knowledge. It's way more free flowing than that. It doesn't need a safety net.

Can't be that simple, can it?

I can't just leave it there. It's not that simple. So often we find ourselves in situations that require a choice between hurting ourselves or hurting someone else, often someone we love. I want a conclusion, I must admit, a guaranteed formula for how to proceed in such situations. I don't have one though; each time seems too different for even a rule of thumb.

Oh. The Golden Rule? It's amazing how such a well known and universally accepted rule is so easily forgotten, and ignored. Maybe that's because in the middle of a crisis we don't even know what we would like to have "others do unto" us in that situation. Our first reaction (okay - *my* first reaction) is not to feel what we truly feel, but to figure it all out instead, ensure our rightness. My mind screams at me in a situation like that, "You don't have time for all that being-in-the-moment crap!! Feel it later. Right now you have to figure this out!!"

So where do we go for guidance? Within, or without? Feeling and intuition type stuff, or concrete knowledge? If I believe I can't be trusted, I'm not likely to go within. Maybe I can suspend the belief that I can't be trusted.

Some people kind of flip out at the suggestion that we can know God's will for us personally by going within and listening. (Oddly, these are often the same people who claim to have Jesus in their heart.) They think that listening from one's own heart and awareness would be the same as deciding for yourself what is good and what is evil. They believe we must always measure our selves against ... (something else), or we'll end up fooling ourselves. They have a point, but it seems obvious to me that there are many measuring sticks - all of which are interpretations of knowledge - *for which we must acquire yet more knowledge and more interpretations so we can know* which is the right stick to stand beside. We are still left with a mere interpretation.

I've noticed there are two kinds of "knowing". There's knowing because of proof, which we could call outer knowing. And what

```
I'll call inner knowing, is something that
we definitely feel at times, even without
good reasons or evidence to back it up.
(But then it starts to go away as soon as
I try to prove it, justify it or keep it.)
I wonder if maybe the fruit (of the tree of
the knowledge of good and evil) symbolizes
that outer knowing that depends on proof.
```

Parrot-Ox

As to people who think listening from your heart is actually just making up your own rules, so to speak, well, they may be doing that very thing themselves. Instead of listening from their heart, they judge different views by various other means to determine truth and falsehood, in order to *decide for themselves* which one to allow to make up the rules for them. I don't think many of them do it simply for the sake of standing in judgement; I'm sure they have a lot of "good reasons" for seeking conclusions. In fact, it's probably quite accurate to say that most people would love nothing more than to *listen* directly to what is from the Original Mind, rather than have to try to *judge* what is. Somewhere along the way they apparently bought into the belief that they can't listen directly.

The main hindrance to that direct kind of listening, I believe, lies in not trusting (and not using) our own hearts. And trusting our own hearts just doesn't seem to happen when avoidance of pain (any kind) is a higher priority than listening.

We are understandably suspicious of direction that makes no sense to us and which seems likely to cause needless suffering if acted upon. But we as adults of the species, are usually equally suspicious when told we can have our cake and eat it too; we might even *assume* that our very own heart is treacherous, if it claims to hear God telling us something we would consider to be just too good to be true. This suspicion is healthy, I think, if it is in balance – as long as it doesn't tip the scales to a conclusion. (Is that a conclusion about conclusions, you ask? Personally, I will likely remain *suspicious* of conclusions, but I don't want to *conclud*e that conclusions are bad – nor does it follow that they are then good, since they're not bad. I want to simply observe, with no judgements.)

I know I'm repeating myself, but if we can accept the insecurity of *not having proof* for backup, then what we end up with is a much deeper and current sense of security in the trustworthiness of the Source of All (yes All – hearts included). Before you made it go away by trying to keep it from going away, isn't that security what you had with your inner knowing? It's a wild Parrot-Ox (as my inner child spells it).

It seems that security, like truth, freedom and love, is a wild thing. They all remain untamed, and uncontained – no matter what. If we *willingly* let them be free, always free to stay or to go, we just might be compatible with them; we're only as free as we freely let anything else be. It is a paradox; to have it you must let it go. (I mean, be letting – present tense.*) What is free is free anyway, so you've got nothing to lose by willingly letting it be what it already is.* Be willingly letting it be always, and in all ways, free. That includes conclusions; just notice the ones that are hanging around and let them be free to come and go. I find they usually become much less conclusive as soon as I become aware of them as conclusions.

I imagine you've noticed the main paradox in this discussion: You can't really decide for yourself until you just listen instead; and you can't really listen until you've decided for yourself to do so.

Here's a regurgitation from a friend of ours on acquired knowledge: "Acquiring knowledge is like acquiring food; eating all we could at every chance we got, was at one point useful for the survival of the species, but in our affluence it'll kill us."

Maybe we have also evolved past a healthy need for knowledge of proof at every chance we get. But quitting the habit is not as easy as it sounds. Just look around you for a minute and see if your eyes, or thoughts for that matter, light on anything that you hold absolutely no beliefs or conclusions about. And notice the belief that we have to hold at least some conclusions in order to function. Just notice it, that's all. Just listen.

And since we're on the topic of paradoxes (which

incidentally, I suspect are the footprints of truth), I want to set something up for your consideration. It is in regard to the depression you spoke of last time we talked. I wonder if you would be interested in an experiment. Next time you feel low, rather than trying to find the cause so you can get rid of it, try to hold it close instead of pushing it away – try to feel more of the depression – don't let any little bit of it go unacknowledged or unfelt. Embrace it, get intimate with it. When I do this with my anger, I usually end up laughing. If I only look for the cause, I just end up angrier. I would be interested to hear how this seemingly contradictory approach works with depression. Maybe "to let it go you must have it" is true as well.

Chapter Three

Tolerance? Justice? All in Time.

Eating and knowledge do have their place, however. Now to the question of tolerance or justice. Where's the balance? How do we handle it? It seems obvious that it would not be intelligent to allow rape and pillage just because we've come to realize we don't have the total knowledge necessary for knowing what's best for everyone in the long run, what the whole big picture is of the highest good for all.

P.S. I've been waiting for a chance to get intimate with my depression, but so far I haven't had any to work with.

Just Is, not Just If

Can we simply make laws, without needing to justify the consequences of breaking them by proving the lawbreakers to be morally wrong? **Do we have to prove a thing is evil** (wrong, bad, faulty….) **before we set a boundary?** I prefer something like this: "The boundary just *is*, right here; not just *if* you‘re wrong. You might even be right to think the way you do, but that doesn't make me wrong and I still don't want your interference – this is the boundary." It doesn't have to become a matter of moral right and wrong, of better or worse. We don't have to take it personally.

Does that seem simplistic? Other issues enter in of course, like: Are black slaves even human? Are unborn children human? Is it okay for animals to suffer from scientific testing in order to protect people from suffering? Torturing terrorists to protect people from suffering? What about killing trees? Eating cows? Lettuce?

Boundaries

Indeed, there are many conflicting views (vegetable rights?). Can we simply stick up for what is important to us without the need to *acquire acceptance of its justification* - without having "a prove-all"?

We *could* set a boundary, or present facts and information, without attacking the opposing view by trying to prove it wrong (as if that would make us automatically right?); but we don't do it that way very often. Attacking or not, we still usually don't *trust our own taste* in the matter; we insist on proof we're right as well. But do we really need justifications? Obviously, you're saying we don't. And I guess we don't need the threats and promises either; in fact, looking at it this way, they are seen to be mere posturing - bluffs and compromises - compensating for a lack of confidence.

But what about issues that require politics, votes - public opinion in order to get those votes for change? The debate over global warming is a good example of the perceived need to point out the error of the opposing view. Here again we've come to the question of who has the truth about what's going on. Who is right? And how can we gain enough proof to know for sure, when there seems to be proof disproving proof all over the place?

To think of living without approval (in any of it's subtle forms) as a prerequisite, thrills me as much as it scares the hell out of me. It feels a little bare-assed, like, "Where's my cover, my backup?"

Trust.

Dear O.

I think most of us believe in God, by some name. Just what God is or does is another matter.

Allow me to get off track a bit here. Why is it a question of creation or evolution, but not both? There has to be something, - some form of energy - that has always been. That something (which I call God) is the source of all else, it's where it all started; so it seems obvious that creation happens. That evolution happens is just as obvious, and you don't even have to go back millions of years or be a scientist to see that; look at the specialized breeds of flowers and fruit trees and livestock for example. Maybe one way God creates is through evolution. I think God is big enough to accommodate both views.

Okay, where was I? Oh yes, trust. If I see, know, feel or believe that God is GOD - all the word implies - how could I not trust that? That kind of God must be a God of total love toward us, for if God is the

All in All, that means we, being part of All, are made up of Godness.

Now here's a big question for those of us who claim to love and trust God: Do I trust God to be GOD? Or is God absolved of evil in the world; do I make God out to be a powerless bystander by saying "God had nothing to do with that"? It seems like a simple question, but think about it. If God is all-powerful, all-knowing and all-present, if God is the All in All, then not only are *we* part of God, but so is everything else - even the things we *"know"* to be evil or shameful. Is God All that Is or just some confused creator we make excuses for?

Any resistance to the idea of trusting comes from a fear of pain, I think. We're afraid we might be that part of God that's on the bottom of the food chain. Before we agree to fully trust, we want proof (reassurance) that God is going to let us hop merrily through the flowers rather than be lunch. We don't want to be a victim, we say; although, often it's being right we want more than anything. Despite the fact it's for security reasons, we'd probably even agree to be "lunch" if we saw it as the best way to be right.

We seek information and the knowledge of proof, because we want to be secure in our rightness. (Quite naturally I suppose - who would want to be wrong?) But if we become dependent on external proof (which is - let's face it - a form of approval) for a sense of well being, it could just be an elaborate route back to victimhood, don't you think? All of a sudden we're back to letting proof do our thinking for us. I want to be informed, but without giving my power away.

Would you rather be a victim than make a mistake and be corrected? I can see that in some areas, that's how I have thought - that I would rather be helpless than be wrong. And though it still pops up at times, the difference is that now I don't justify it like I used to by thinking like this: "I'm suffering now but that's okay because I won't be blamed (see, I can't help it because …) and being blameless will save me from suffering in the future." But I find it is always the present; whenever I get to the future it's still the present after all. (Duh.) I can only choose in the moment. And besides, *why do we think the future is so much more important than the present anyway?*

I was being helpless now so I could be right; and why do I want to be right? To have some control, so I will be safe and non-victimized in the future. Is it intelligent to be the thing you don't want in order to save yourself from being that? Hmmm. That was meant to be rhetorical (but if paradoxes are footprints …). Maybe I'm on to something, like with embracing the depression or anger. I guess the difference is whether it is done consciously or not. Also, it is not actually "embracing" if it is done for the purpose of getting rid of the thing; embracing is something done for the sake of intimacy, of getting to know it, with love. Like they say, what you resist will persist. I have to own it first; I have to see what I'm being before I can quit being that. (groan, sigh)

Is our responsibility something to do with how we respond to "what is"? I think if we respond like a victim we get to be one. In that case, even **if I'm going down anyway** (if that happens to be "what is"), **I may as well do it like a hero.**

I'm reminded of the statement "happiness is a state of mind". (Then victimhood or heroism would naturally be as well.) Apparently it is a choice. I asked U. for input on the subject.

Re: State of Mind

First you have to be willing to suspend the belief – suspend, not exchange remember – that it isn't really entirely a choice. Actually allow the possibility that it is a choice. Happiness is a choice. From there it's new – unknown. There is no formula. (Before going further, I need to throw in another possibly confusing qualifier. It's about the word choice. What I mean by "choice", when I say state of mind is a choice, is not quite the same as decision making with regard to results. It's choice with surrender. It's our choice but not our results, since ultimately the results of our choices always lead to awareness of oneness, whether we like it or not. We can create in accord, in the flow of oneness, or out of accord – that's our choice too. And if we choose to be passive spectators rather than participate, even then we are inevitably creating. How we look at it is how it is; that is what we experience. When we see what's what, choice comes so naturally that it feels like it's already been made.)

So, choosing happiness as your state of mind is really just being willing to love *what is*. What I mean is, choosing to get intimate with what is, rather than resisting it and trying to avoid the pain of it. You don't have to like it in order to do this. Just watch and feel, **and let it be.** There's nothing you need to do about the pain or pleasure of what is. And you **don't need to know** what it means for the future.

If you feel it (the pain or pleasure) and be with it, you can see it clearly. But if you hold onto or push away the pleasure or pain, there will be conflict, which seriously hinders happiness and clear seeing. It must be always free – not just free to "make up its mind" – but always free to come or go. *If you can observe it and leave it alone, the rest will take care of itself.*

Let yourself just feel what you feel, without settling on any ideas of what it means, then the clear seeing moves in and any other kind of action you take will also be intelligent. But you won't really think of it as being intelligent action; it'll be too obvious, like moving out of the way of a falling rock. You might take action, but that doesn't mean you will resist the fact that the situation is there to deal with. The conflict, the struggle, the suffering – the unhappiness – is in the resistance. It's always a struggle to refuse love.

Experience and Time

I doubt it's necessary, but I'd like to clarify my use of the word evil. The knowledge of good and evil is about what is good and what isn't. When I say "evil" I just mean what isn't good. (Take a slightly naughty or false thing far enough and we call it evil.)

One begins to realize knowledge in general comes into this discussion as well as knowledge about morals. For example, someone has knowledge which they believe would be beneficial for humanity and soon there is a group spreading the word, pushing this information. If more time and information proves that to follow through on this knowledge would actually be detrimental, we might go so far as to call that particular knowledge evil, because it caused suffering and depravity. It didn't start out as a moral issue, so why did it get turned into one? What was the thinking behind that switch? Something like this maybe: "Suffering is bad so what ever causes it must be bad too." Then a little more thought and, "Oh, but actually, some suffering brings about great insight and healing so then that suffering is good." Since we judge a thing according to its end result, it's no wonder we want to know the future.

Enter Time.

From past experience (knowledge) we can make educated guesses. We try to know the future from the past, which we only have partial knowledge about, so yes - it is just guessing. And the present? We don't really seem to give it much importance, which is odd when you think of it since it's the only part of time we can ever experience. (The past is a memory of an experience, and the future is however we see it - a hope or a dread of an experience.) What about knowing the *present* from the past? Another guess.

Can we know enough about the past (an eye blink ago or a big bang ago) to know enough about the future to say for sure what is good or evil? Well, it seems we can't, no matter how tempted we are to keep on trying to prove we can. We cannot prove what will turn out to be good or bad in the future.

There are, however, some things from the past I sure don't want in the future, but old habits die hard; I find myself still trying to learn enough to ensure that it won't happen again, still trying to find conclusive security. On the other hand, I guess learning from our mistakes does not necessarily equate with needing guarantees that there'll be no repeats.

I'm reminded of a little plaque I used to have:

Good judgment comes from experience.

Experience comes from bad judgment.

It seemed appropriate to leave it behind last time I moved. Is there a plaque that says what comes from good judgment?

Time Experiment

Imagine there is no tomorrow. Better yet, no next moment in time – on any level. Anywhere. Ever. For anyone. I realize this is asking a lot, but try. No heaven, no hell. No future acknowledgements of any kind. The idea of rewards or punishment is a moot topic. No karma either, no next life, no consequences. Nothing but here, now, this moment, today. Go ahead, imagine it; you won't get stuck there.

Now, would there be any point in knowing good from evil? True from false? You might want to say or do certain things *just because that's how you are*, but you wouldn't need reassurances about how things would turn out in the end – not if this very moment is all there is to it. You would do what you felt like with no fear of the consequences of being wrong, nor anticipation of rewards for being right. (Are you surprised at how much fun good deeds are this way?)

When you can, stay in that feeling of no judgements or consequences for a moment. Now, how much can you worry about the future? Can you worry about anything at all without bringing consequences and results (time) into it? I can't.

Look at it another way. If you didn't worry about the future (on any level, remember), would you worry about knowing good from evil?

Backwards

It was really tough for me to suspend my belief in the future long enough to feel what it would be like without it. What an experiment! You could smile at anyone you felt like without concern for what it might lead to, or give care to war torn orphans of all kinds, even if it wouldn't make a bit of difference. You could be alone on a mountain top or have a lot of sex, or pecan pie. Or not. It would be life without "shoulds" or "good enough reasons". Suspending belief in the past as well, is an added dimension.

The attempt to know right from wrong does seem to be interdependent with time. If we weren't so bothered about what the future holds, we wouldn't be so bothered about good-and-true versus evil-and-false; and the other way around; if we weren't worried about knowing true from false, we wouldn't be worried about what time will tell. No worries about what's good or not, equals no worries about outcomes. (Do time and knowledge exist only as fuel for each other?) Another way to put it could be: A time paradigm is dependent on the intention to gain proof of a justified sense of security.

Our belief in time gives us a reason to care about true and false, more and less - essentially, a reason to judge between good and evil. My guess, is that humanity will seek security in established knowledge until the end of time. There's nothing ominous about that; I simply see the end of time as we know it, a likely outcome to the end of the search for (and dependence on) tangible evidence of justification for psychological security - in other words, the search for proof we're alright.

I'm sure you are aware of some of the interesting information that science and technology are bringing us regarding time, like how it's not as predictable as we once thought. Neither is matter for that matter; it's mostly empty space apparently, for one thing. Quantum theory is very interesting. Maybe it really is all backwards like you said; our thoughts and feelings affect - actually *effect* - what happens, rather than our thoughts and feelings being an effect of what happens. But that's getting back to science of some kind, and I'm not done looking at things from this other perspective yet.

Chapter Four

Kingdoms

Dear O.,

We talked awhile back about this and I'd like to explore further the meaning of the Kingdom of God, or Kingdom of Heaven. And what about Jesus? Does he have anything to do with the subject of the knowledge of good and evil?

There seems to be some debate on whether the terms Kingdom of God and Kingdom of Heaven are interchangeable or mean different things. Some believe the Kingdom of Heaven is the organic/material outer manifestation of the Kingdom of God; the Kingdom of God then being the spiritual/ nonmaterial inner aspect. In other words, what is 'out there' is what is 'in there'; as within, so without. Seems to go with sowing what you want to reap, and the Golden Rule as well. The terms are regularly used interchangeably however, even in the Bible; but when I've come across either term, it almost always seems to be considering the inner aspect, which suits this discussion just fine.

"But seek ye first the Kingdom of God, and his righteousness; and all these things shall be added unto you." (Matt 6:330) Where do we start with that? (Right off I'd like to note that the little phrase "and his righteousness" is often taken as an invitation to judge - to seek and/or give approval. You'd be right if you guessed I'm not presently going along with that.)

Seek first, not second or later when conditions are right in the future sometime, or after we have proof that we know for sure exactly what the Kingdom of God is. And what are all these things that will be added? Of course, you'll have to read it for your own interpretation of the context, but to me it seems they are things we hope will provide us with security - assurances that we will avoid suffering in our future. "These things" are not what we are to seek first, no matter how distractingly reasonable, good and necessary they are. Just because they are necessary doesn't mean they come first. (Suspend *that*!)

The more I think about it, and read and talk about it, the more I come back to the ideas we already touched on about conscience and intuition, that inner knowing. If we're happy with the outer kind of knowing we can go on believing things through a process of becoming convinced, because they've been "proven" to be true. It's the mind that does the proving, *"So pick a belief you like and let the mind justify it. It will. That's what it does"*. (Quote from U.) I'd say that usually we don't even pick the belief for ourselves; we've let someone or something else do that for us. We end up believing a lot of things that trouble us.

Then there are the times our senses give us information that shakes our previous beliefs. If at some point we get enough information, we might call it proof; but we're still bound by the process, sort of like a puppet - we can't know it until it's been approved.

With the inner knowing there is no approval, no back-up. *Except directly from GOD* - you know, if it's true and everything that inner knowing is actually from God and to be trusted. And that's what I'm wondering - which way is more trustworthy?

I mean, if they don't seem to agree, which one is the rule and which is the tool? Of course they are both from God, of GOD, but is one meant to guide the other? At this point it still seems ludicrous a lot of the time, yet I keep coming back to inner knowing as the primary guiding principle. Not *instead* of knowledge of evidence - for sure not - because I think they work together.

There is apparently no proof, no formulas or guarantees; we just have to take that leap and find out. The hard part for me is **to be willing to make mistakes** (and welcome correction) as I learn to listen first to that inner guidance. Maybe this is where pure intent comes in, rather than intent with the condition of approval.

We make mistakes all the time with the use of outer knowledge. Why is that so much more acceptable? It's like we want proof that *other people can acknowledge*, so we won't be blamed for mistakes. "You poor thing. You did all you could; it's not your fault." And why don't we take it as correction when we experience mistakes? Why do we choose to believe it's right for us to suffer? **Why do we prefer to be helpless rather than to be corrected?** I have noticed that I've often been more inclined to take the suffering of consequences as though I'm guilty or as a victim, rather than as a student; I've taken correction (from life, events, people) as punishment or attack, rather than as a bit of advice from All That Is.

When I talk about "outer knowing" here, I don't mean the same thing as I would mean if I said "seeing what is." Seeing what is, as an apparent fact, is one thing; it's what intelligent action springs from. Labelling what you see in such a way that confines and limits it to a conclusion, is quite another thing. Outer knowing boxes and labels, telling you what it means (for future reference of course - why else?), but the trouble with that is, that all those conclusion boxes are managed by Would-be, Should-be and their cousin Could-be. Not from the same branch as What-is.

Anyway, as I said, I come back to conscience, or inner knowing. (I think you understand that I don't in any way mean a guilty feeling about breaking the rules, when I say conscience. I'm referring to private, personal, direct communication with God.) My approach is that this inner country is where to seek the Kingdom of God, or Heaven; this kingdom is where life "works". I don't have proof this perception is correct, but I trust God to show me in a way I can understand whenever I'm making a mistake.

There will never be a "good" time, when taking responsibility will be easier or better somehow. If I wait till I know for sure that I know how to take the leap, I never will leap.

Now to - "what about Jesus?" I have always had a lot of questions about Jesus: who is he, what did he do exactly, what does he do now, what is so important about Jesus dying on the cross? "He gave his life to save sinners and rose again on the third day", doesn't really tell me much.

There are a lot of different answers, besides the various learned responses, pat answers - even among those who use the same sources of information. (I suppose that goes without saying.) I'm just going to skip to my main question.

Why do we need to know? WHY do we need to know? Why do WE need to know? Why do we NEED to know? Why do we need to KNOW? (Lately that really is my main question.)

I don't know what you think on this topic, but here is a bit of what I have discussed with myself. If Jesus came and did his thing for us, well - it's done! So let's get on with it. (I'm not saying "let's stop wondering".) Don't you think that's what he had in mind - that we move on to what he made possible for us? Even if we've never heard of him, it's done and it's possible. If we're going to stick with the translation that no one can "come unto the Father but by me" (Jesus), we may as well act like we believe it and get on with coming unto the Father; Jesus made it so we can. Maybe I'm missing the whole point, by thinking the whole point ***is*** to "come unto the Father". But isn't that what it's all about? (The Father, I think, refers to God - who is GOD, the Original Mind, All That Is. Would you agree? In another time and place the name might have been translated as "the Mother".) My take on this, is that coming unto the Father/ Kingdom of God is essentially an attitude of surrender.

What do you think; did Jesus change something or just show the way - was he a demonstration of how to be human? An interesting question, but on the other hand, it doesn't really matter, does it? (If you think it does matter, I'd be interested to hear your thoughts on that.) As I see it, either way, he fixed it - whether we just needed to be shown or whether something needed to be changed. Maybe it was both, but the important part is that *coming "unto the Father" is possible for us.*

Is this coming unto the Father basically an attitude of willingness to communicate with God directly - rather than as though we are separated? Is it basically to accept our oneness? "Seek ye first ..." may simply be to give *primary* importance to the art of learning how to listen for ourselves, to what righteousness is according to God; surrendering unconditionally to God the All in All, rather than to approval or fear.

Some would wonder if that is bypassing Jesus, making insignificant his death on the cross. But if Jesus is no more God then the rest of us, then what he did is between him and God, just like the rest of us; and if he is God, then how could it be bypassing if it's God we're surrendering to? Besides, it should be noted that Jesus is not still up on the cross. He moved on, and possibly we would do well to follow his example.

Maybe what Jesus did was something to do with aligning our consciences with the mind of God. Or maybe he just showed us some possibilities and left the means: the Comforter, Counsellor, Advocate - various translations of the Greek "Parakletos", I believe - which refers to the Holy Spirit. (John 14:26). I also find it interesting that Jesus considered his disciples better off without his physical presence, since it meant they could have the indwelling Holy Spirit instead. (John 16:7) Whatever and however all that may be, Jesus did what he did and *"It is finished."*

And I think I'm finished for now too, in spite of all the new questions this has provoked. You mentioned something about a journal you are keeping; I'd like to see some of that, if it's something you would share.

CHAPTER FIVE

Chronicle Of The Cricket

This journal is about my working relationship with the cricket, although relationship may not be quite the right word because it's not just a point of connection. Besides being relative to each other we are also inseparable, indivisible. To consider one is to consider the other, not by association only, but directly as well.

The cricket is what others might call intuition, or the Holy Spirit, higher Self, Nagual, inner knowing, gut feeling, conscience, the observer; these and probably many other terms, mean different things to different people. I just use the one I like best, the cricket, for this part of us that knows how it all works together for the highest good for all. In particular, **that** it all works together – naturally – there's only one of us here. (I don't think that "I am GOD", as in all that GOD is; it's more like "All that I am is GOD".) I expect Jiminy Cricket was more than just a conscience for Pinocchio. Although, an **unconditioned** conscience may be the same thing as "the cricket".

I get to a certain point where I may as well start all over again as keep on deleting and changing; this is but the latest Cricket Journal. I still don't know what it is about the last one that doesn't feel right. Anyway, here I go again, on my favourite subject.

Not that long ago, I came to the crux of the matter; I found life to be pointless and not really worth the bother if a total connection is nothing but wishful thinking. It's all meaningless; a delusional pretense of knowing how to live – just a bunch of fear-filled attachments to various types of approval – that's all it ends up being if true unity is not possible, **no matter what I give, or get, or become.**

Since then I've taken some leaps I couldn't quite manage before I had this nothing-to-lose frame of mind. With it I can see that anything I seemingly stand to lose if I'm wrong about trusting the cricket, is after all, only some part of that meaningless life I don't want anymore.

When I try to talk about this, people often tend to think I need anti-depressants and that I should get help. But far from being depressed or suicidal, I find that having nothing to lose is actually quite light and even exciting because freedom is only limited by how much I cling to anything I don't want to lose. (A person in prison even, could be more free than someone with civil rights, a family, home and good job.)

One of the first questions was: How can I know what the cricket is saying? I've noticed that if I require a system, a formula for knowing, then I don't know and I won't know; it is one of those things that only functions in freedom. If I'm really letting it be free, I don't require it to stay on a marked path. And of course, without a marked path I'm left with not knowing how to know, and when I am being okay with that, then the cricket can talk to me.

Actually, it's a silly, ego oriented question (How can I know?). It's beside the point as well, because the communication itself is really the thing I want; I don't need to know HOW to know what the communication is if I already got it. And I can't get it unless I see it as free, rather than something to control. I suppose the ego doesn't think anything is valid or useful unless it can be summoned.

Today I came across a page of ranting and raving that I think fits in here:

> *Just because some spiritual leader, somebody who is supposed to know, says something like, "spending money creates a vacuum" – it doesn't make it true. And we're told to "believe it" and we can do or have anything we want. Maybe it's true, but I don't know and I can't just choose to believe it. I can choose to act like I believe it, but I don't really – not till I see for myself that that is how it works. And, I've already experimented with trying to fool myself into believing.*
>
> *Days like today – when I really want to know how it all works – it just doesn't help to hear stuff like, "Everything is an illusion, anything and everything is potentiality until you manifest something by giving it your thoughts, intention and attention." Or, "Meditate and find the silence, the space between your thoughts, for that is where all things are created." Sometimes I*

even think I know what they mean by that, and intellectually I can support it with the knowledge that it can even be backed up with some science. But in the throes of a bad day what fucking good is it? The message becomes, "So, Stupid, stop making a bad day for yourself!" Obviously I would stop if I had some idea of how to stop. Is there no such thing as practical help and advice; does it all have to come from somebody who is calmly telling you things as though they have no idea what a bad day is like?

I'm already starting to feel better, now since I quit trying to feel better. I thought, screw this, why should I struggle with it? Who really cares if I feel like shit, and who should judge, as long as they don't have to be around me, or hear about it? Am I a failure for not being happy and content and wealthy? Who says? And would I be a nicer person, or any less a failure if I did struggle with it? It seems to be expected and is quite respectable; it makes me quite 'nice' (non-threatening) to be stressed and struggling. But who cares? So what? I quit! I'd rather sit in my depression, this hole of frustration, than struggle with it anymore.

Actually I'm pretty happy at the moment, not struggling with my unhappiness. Hmmm ...Okay, so what just happened there? I quit struggling. I quit trying to feel better, to measure up. I quit trying to make what-is out to be something it is not. I quit avoiding the pain.

I also had some ideas about what happiness is supposed to be like. I remember now that happiness is one of those things that doesn't need a "because"; it really is independent of what is going on. (This, from a frustrated, bad day person.) And it doesn't have to pass any inspections to be valid as true happiness. You can't delude yourself into believing that you're happy or unhappy; there's no one else who can set you straight on that one. You can call it anything you like, but you can't really believe you feel happy when you just don't. Of course, you surely can believe that you should *feel happy, or unhappy as the case may be.*

So, does the same principal hold for things like money? I wonder. If I quit struggling with money issues will money quit being an issue? To me, deciding to go into debt seems like a struggle for sure, but what about little things, everyday? Like new socks and underwear when I don't really need any yet, or extra gas for the scenic route. Just do it, instead of struggle with it?

There's this balancing act I always do, and I know how I learned it, but that is beside the point now. I have a history of struggling like this: "Will I have enough later if I spend this now?" Even when I have had tons of money I have done this. Like as if I can know the future, I use all the knowledge I have acquired to calculate the answer. I guess I'm a slow learner, but finally I have noticed that neither correct nor incorrect calculations have ever seemed to affect my success rate all that much.

I won't spend for the sake of creating a vacuum, as tempting as that is to the fearful part of me that clings to the illusion of control. It thinks a big enough, or sure enough vacuum would render the cricket unnecessary. But it's the cricket that knows where, what and when things give that meaningful sense to life. So I'll try spending for the cricket, whenever it feels right instead of just when it calculates right. I want to find out for myself.

So, how do I know if it's the cricket? Maybe it's just a fear. In this I have found that I need to be willing to make mistakes. If I go by what a fear is telling me, it'll be a mistake – but mistakes are okay – it's one way to learn. If I'm afraid to make a mistake, it's going to be hard to get me to try anything new; it'll be hard to show me that what I'm doing isn't really working very well, that there's a better way. Like my dog; if he knows he's not bad just because he's wrong, then even when he's an old dog he can keep on learning "new tricks" with ease. I'm not bad when I'm wrong; I'm just mistaken, incorrect.

I found some huge fears all around this issue. I notice ways that I have bought into that old "you've made your bed, so sleep in it" idea, like as if I had one chance to do something right and I don't get any more. Apparently I'm not the only one. I know better, but unconsciously my mind has been very diligent in support of the belief that mistakes have irreversible consequences, that to make a mistake which requires correction, is equivalent to irrevocable condemnation – if I'm wrong, I'm done for. But actually, this is hardly ever the case. (Considering that we are eternal beings, could it

ever be the case?) Outrageous as it seems to say, video games may help to displace this collective unconscious belief, because if you make a mistake you just start again.

This question (Is it a fear or is it the cricket?) seems to be the biggest one for me. I second guess my self at every turn. Coming to the point of having nothing to lose was a big turning point in my approach, and I became aware of another aspect of that when I started asking myself if there is anything that I can actually **possess**, if there is any situation or thing that cannot be lost. I found, the answer is no. I can lose any of my abilities or possessions. Loved ones can die or withdraw from me. I can lose my body, my memory, and my influence; it can all be snuffed out. Of course there is the part of me that is eternal and indestructible, but that's not "mine" – it just is. So is love.

So yes, that was a turning point; surrender became much simpler. Having nothing to lose is having nothing to fear, and having no fear is freedom. When I am realizing that I actually do have nothing to lose (that nothing of real value **can** be lost and also, anything I can lose was only ever mine to use – to enjoy for awhile), then I am definitely more willing to take a chance on the cricket – to possibly **make mistakes and be corrected**.

∽∘∽

Today there's that how to know thing... **again.** Why do I need to know if it's a fear or if it's the cricket? Well for reassurance of course, but why do I even need that reassurance? Being reassured doesn't make me right, or safe. In fact, if I ever came across one, I actually ought to refuse any sort of guarantee about this, because conclusions are stops and restrictions, they obstruct the flow.

I see I haven't been "letting it be free". I've been trying to figure out how to control outcomes instead. Why? Fear of some kind of pain, I guess. I must be thinking I have something to lose again.

So, if I let this whole cricket connection **be free**, I simply observe that I don't know, and I don't make a judgment about that; I don't try to contain it in a box of "I should know" or "I need to know". And of course I don't pretend to know. Instead, I suspend the belief that I need to know. It doesn't matter if it makes no sense to me; right now I just need to be in the moment with no judgment. When I get out of the way like this, the channel of communication is clear.

twinges

the twinges of fearlessness I felt today
were not like in the old days of naively
walking through walls bravely
since no one I trusted ever told me I couldn't

today I felt that lion-heartedness
with something more like innocence
a decided lack of that pretense
which naivety doesn't even know is expected

Be willing to make mistakes and be corrected – that's getting to the fun part: the communicating. **Being corrected is a communication**. I kind of feel that the cricket is a part of GOD that communicates, not the part that does the material correction or confirmation of the reception of that communication. (But it's all One so I guess that's neither here nor there.)

Correction and confirmation on a material, organic level is very helpful in the learning process. However, this tangibly observable feedback is delayed; it's kind of a detour from the instant and direct feedback of the cricket. So, do I really need this to be a process? Why not just trust the cricket? I want to, so what are the unconscious fears that hold me back? (Nothing to lose – remember?)

One other disadvantage I see in relying on material feedback is that it tends to promote the inclination to look "outward" rather than "inward" for confirmation, as if something **else** must prove I'm right or approve of me before I'm okay – before what I think, say, do, believe, feel, is valid enough to be true to. But my feelings don't need endorsement.

If I insist on proof I'm right (approval in some

form from people, events or evidence, phenomena, visions, ascended masters …) **before** I am willing to follow through on my intention to listen to the cricket, I'm dangerously close to choosing victimhood; I'm giving away my power – now it's up to some **other** to be or do something in order that I can be okay with what I feel. To rely on outward confirmation implies an underlying belief of separateness – me, and the validater(s) of me.

I'm all for being informed, but I don't want to create limitations by coming to conclusions. The obvious assumption lying in the perceived need for conclusive evidence, is that what ever is other than the proven right is automatically wrong, or less desirable. When I have learned the right way to do something, I have limited myself to doing it that way to the same extent that I am convinced that it is The Right Way.

Though it is apparently necessary for survival, what we've learned from the past or think it means for the future, is what can limit us. But if we are right here right now, accepting no conclusions, we're unrestricted. Hearing the cricket is right now. What is in this moment is, "How do I feel right now?" I mean right now, not the result of right now; not, "what will prove to be best in the end for me to feel right now?" There are no shoulds involved in hearing the cricket.

Any conclusions I have agreed to abide by

are only hindrances to my full presence in this moment. Conclusions exclude much of what IS. It's harder to surrender the outcome when I think I already know what the possibilities are. To conclude is to exclude. It's very limiting. So why do I keep finding myself trying to **know** the future before I decide how I should feel? There's that paradox thing again; to have it you must let it go – not control it.

Where I'm at on this at the moment is something like this: The cricket tells us what "flows" the best for each one of us in any given moment. There are no rules or rationale we can follow intellectually; the cricket speaks to us in the moment, through our feelings, and I mean our **feelings in and about the moment**, not about the future or the past. ~ Ohh. Maybe that is the distinction I've been wanting to make between feeling and emotion: we have an **emotion** because of what something means (even though it is we ourselves who give everything whatever meaning it holds for us – consciously or otherwise – according to our beliefs and conditioning); whereas **feeling** just is, with no justification, no reason, no "because". ~ What flows for me, is naturally going to be flowing the best for everything else as well, since we're all the same stuff, the same one.

"This above all: To thine own self be true, and it must follow, as night the day, thou canst not then be false to any man." And speaking of Shakespeare: "To be or not to be, . . ." **I can't wait until I am before I choose to be, for it's only in the choosing, that I am.** That blows my mind, over and over again.

The cricket's favourite food seems to be unadulterated me. Sans ego. (What I mean by the word, ego, is that part of me that seeks security in proofs, certainty, guarantees; in a word – control.) One of the best ways I've found for preparing this dish, is what-ising, which can expose and filter the ego because it's not about conclusions. What-ising is just plain observing **without** judgment: not to see that, "it is blue," but rather, "it appears blue to me in this moment," allowing that I don't know for certain. In other words, I just feel what I feel, and see what I see, even if it goes against apparent facts. The apparent facts are also part of what is. I can take into account that it's labelled pink and everyone else might see it as pink, while I still see blue – but I don't draw conclusions about the truth of either colour.

So then it follows that, for example, if I see my friend do something that appears to betray my trust, and I simply what-is it, I don't come to conclusions about my friend's intentions or loyalty. If I still feel like being with my friend the same as before, I do, in spite of the "proof" he's no good. I see that what is, is that I saw him do such and such, and also that I don't know why. (I can't know what went on in his mind.) I don't know what his actions (or thoughts) mean; I can only speculate. And I may have a strong desire to speculate if I still have an attachment to proof of security. Once again, the fear of the unknown; but each time I face it, it's easier the next time.

Any **meaning** I have attached to the past is part of what is now, if I still hold to that, so that comes into what-ising too sometimes. Also, the thoughts I'm thinking are part of what is, even if they are about what was or might be. What IS, is anything in this moment – it's what's happening. I may as well face it and see what it is. It's not something already done and set in stone, nor is there any point in worrying that it **might** happen – it already is happening.

Drawing conclusions from the past or trying to know the future, will obscure the clear seeing that is only in the present moment – that clear seeing that inevitably gives rise to intelligent action. And, if I go back to needing proof that I'm seeing correctly, the ego (or maybe it's the mind – doesn't matter) starts taking control again, diluting the cricket's favourite dish.

(sidetrack note: I don't altogether agree with the idea that the ego/mind is some sort of blight to be overcome. I think of it more like a good Border Collie – it needs a job or it'll cause trouble. It'll take over and decide how to do things if nobody else is going to. You need to play with it, or it will play with you.)

It might go another way, too. I might get the feeling that I no longer want to associate with this person, (or keep the job, go to the party…) in spite of the "proofs" and all the good reasons why I should. What is, is that I feel this way, as well as that I don't know why. I don't need to have reasons (a great shock to the teachers from the old school). Besides, allowing a feeling to be with me does not mean I have agreed to act on it. ~ Oh my … I think I better write that again; a light just came on. ~ Allowing a feeling to be with me does not mean that I am bound to act on it; **I am free to feel what I feel and see what I see despite what it might turn out to mean.** Getting to know a feeling, does not make me obligated to find out what it means and what to do about it. Nor are my feelings a dictatorship – I have free will.

How do I learn this language? How do I interpret my impressions of what the cricket is communicating? Can this language be so clear and refined that I don't need any other confirmation? In fact, is **it** the confirmation of all else?

I got a helpful clue the other day (after I finally asked). The little phrase that came to mind was, "I will tell me in a way that I understand." I will tell me… So I can quit looking for messages that I need to translate. It will be put to me in a way that is meant for **me** to understand, in a way I would use to jog my own memory.

I might get material clues as well, but I will still need to interpret those clues all by myself, inwardly, alone. It's for the masses, this unity, but oh so personal.

When I have dared to entrust my feelings with and to All That Is, dared to feed the cricket enough of it's favourite food (be true to myself), it gets stronger. It's sort of more like a dragon than a cricket when fed consistently. The very ferocious impersonality of it gives it an eternally personal effect; it has no stake in the outcome, and it is an impartial observer that knows and will communicate with me about what's best for all, which always happens to be the same thing that will work best for me personally. **Seeing** what is, is cricket feed – **loving** it takes a dragon (which functions in the voluntary surrender that is total freedom).

And using the word "love" causes me to want to write a bit about that too. I don't know much about what love actually is; I suppose that's because it's so unlimited. Maybe true love is seeing someone or some thing for what it really is and letting it be. Just letting them be that. I don't mean we should stand in its way if what it is will rip us to shreds. I just mean respect it, treat it like it's behaving according to what it is.

I think I've found the thing that wasn't setting right in my last cricket journal. It's about what I called dreaming, which I think is pretty much the same thing as what has also been called positive thinking, creative visualization, programming the universe, praying, and so on; basically, to create or influence your reality, choosing what you want to see happen.

It's not that now I think this is just a bunch of woo-woo. Science shows us that everything is connected; we can influence an object's behaviour through the attention of our minds, for instance. Even at great distances this has apparently been proven possible and somewhat predictable. A basic study of Quantum physics shows a fundamental order of things that implies that we are creators of our own personal reality. I notice that observations from metaphysical, spiritual and philosophical perspectives seem to coincide, as well as observations from my own life.

I still think that it is my part to dream, to take my pick; but now I try to remember to first let go of the string to the outcome. It seems that the surrender comes first. In fact it must naturally do so if we are choosing freedom, for if one is living free (letting everything be free and therefore being free oneself) then one is naturally surrendered already.

And then there's no avoiding this: if one has surrendered all outcomes already, then whatever outcome is happening is okay. We still breath and die and laugh and cry, but there's peace in it all. Evidently, peace is another thing that doesn't need a reason; it doesn't need justification in order to be experienced.

I see that surrender could be another word for love: letting it be free (surrender), happens when we treat it like it's behaving according to what it is in that moment (love). In that sense, I can even love the lion (or the rapist ...) that has attacked me – even while I kill it, or am killed myself. I don't have to justify anything first before I can be true to myself, whatever that is in the moment.

This type of love/surrender is obviously not an agreement that I have no choice but to be a prisoner, a martyr, a victim. It is not fearful or resigned submissiveness, nor is it an attempt to gain control over where blame is laid (presumably not on the victim). Instead, it is the giving up of ultimate possession and control; it's a voluntary relinquishment – easy, because it's no longer about the outcome. It is about what I am; it's about love. Fervid surrender; there is no reluctance because it is not sacrifice. Love – "just is, not just if". Being true to myself, I am naturally and automatically true to all else.

So my question now is, if whatever is happening is okay, then when or why would I ever want to change what is happening? Would I just be interfering? And here's a question that has a cricket feel to it: **Could** I interfere, intentionally or otherwise? Ultimately? I kind of doubt it. The ability to create my own reality is only an implication of a higher order, an all inclusive order.

So, when would I ever want or need to change what is happening? Well, the fact of the matter is that when it comes right down to it, it really only matters whether it's in the flow or not – if the cricket is happy or not, if it's in accord with All, or not. It doesn't seem to matter **what** is happening; if I've got that happy-cricket feeling then I really do believe that it's somehow okay. (I know, onlookers might just call that cold hearted, unfeeling.) I don't need to know **how** it could be, before something can be perfect in the big scheme of things. Perfection isn't dependent on my knowledge.

Being in the flow **does not mean that I just take whatever comes** without feeling what I feel. It's more like I trust that I will feel what I need to feel for direction, and so I am ready and willing to act on it. (If there's to be no action, why worry about guidance? Guidance for what?) Seems like a bit of a conundrum – I only get in the way when I try to figure out what it means, yet if it means taking action I am a blockage if I don't act. But if I just take **notice** of when I start thinking that I have to figure things out, then I can quit it. That noticing gives me the opportunity to get back in touch with my feelings. Hard to feel my feelings when I think I have to know everything. When I feel what I feel and see what I see, then intelligent action happens automatically and spontaneously. Like swerving to avoid oncoming traffic, it will seem too obvious to particularly be called intelligent.

I don't have to know where the flow is going in order to be in it. Go with the flow instead of the struggle. The struggle I am refusing – **not** choosing – is in trying to figure out what will be best. It's a great struggle to have to always be right.

Again, why would I ever change what is happening? Another way to look at it is that we are creating constantly anyway. Whatever the content of my consciousness is – that's what I will automatically, naturally be creating. Wittingly, or witlessly. In that case it's more appropriate to redress my consciousness than to attempt to effect any outward changes first. Always from the inside out it seems.

Noteworthy here is that the content of my total "consciousness" includes what I am conscious of and also what I am unconscious of. Somebody ought to make up another word …

More insight from the dog: He's always ready to play, and I am always telling him what the game is (wittingly or witlessly). I might not mean to tell him to go dig the garden up until I'm ready to throw a ball, but that's the message he got. Always playing the game I am presenting – consciously or not.

Dogs communicate a lot with mind pictures. If I call him to me but imagine the thing I don't want – him looking at me and going the other way, for example – he may be confused as to what I mean. He might show me that he thought I meant for him to come after he does some other stuff. If I accept that without correcting my presentation, he'll give me more of the same – he aims to please.

The analogy breaks down here somewhere, but I think the universe communicates and plays in much the same way, always playing the game I present – giving me what I have in my mind, not necessarily what I "had in mind". When I am aware of consciousness that isn't working, I can change my mind picture – change the game. In this way I can say "take me there", and the universe does. But it's still up to me to say yes and hang on for the ride. I notice I often say "yes but", or "yes maybe", and look for a good place to land in case I want to bail off instead. (Even philosophizing, I end up back on a horse… Now where's my dog?)

The dog works as a model of the universe for me, and at the same time is a great mirror that's in my face a lot. I am the dog, as well as the dog handler. (The Zen of Dog?)

I need to ponder more on that whole dreaming thing. It may be that I'm just scared of my own power and I'm looking for a way to be a helpless victim instead; but I do wonder about it because sometimes to purposely dream **a particular out-**

come seems almost too invasive, pushy, demanding, judgemental – controlling. It somehow feels petty, and kind of phoney. At the same time it seems to be a thing we have the ability to do, so I don't want to just write it off either.

Ahh… once again this reminder: I see that I make it into a confusion for myself just by not listening **first** to the cricket; I start trying to figure things out first, and then listen. Will I **always** need these reminders? Oh, and again, there's more … back to this: **~ Dreaming is for my insides.** It's for me, my heart and soul, my consciousness. My creative power is **for my own evolving. ~** It's in this way that we create our reality, and the evolving of the world around us as well. It's living from the inside out. Seek **first** the Kingdom of God, **and then** all these other things shall be added … What is "in there" first, will be "out there".

So when something or someone out there is upsetting me, I can take that as an indication, a reflection of a problem area I have within myself that I need to address – hard as that may be to take. (Now **that** sets much better with the cricket.) If someone in my life seems to always be complaining about how I do things, for example, it could be a reflection of how I do the same thing to others myself, or maybe it's about how I do it **to** myself. I might want to say "she shouldn't do that", so I can turn that around to "maybe I shouldn't do that", or maybe to "she **should** do that". There's a lot of ways to turn things around, looking from all sides till I hit the nerve. Very scary, and very hard to look at, but it feels right. That outward physically observable stuff will happen naturally and spontaneously in accord with whatever the energy of my attention is. If I'm dishonest say, with myself or others, guess what I'll see when I look out there.

~o~

Had a struggling day yesterday. I have had this idea that I should "rise above" the situation, make it smell like a bed of roses ... Make it into something that to me right now it is not. (I've been through this hOw many times now?) I have not been exercising the dragon – I have not been loving what is. If it's shit, I don't love it by saying it could-be, should-be a rose garden – something other than it is. Instead, when I respect it enough to treat it like it is behaving according to what it is, then I am as free as I let it be. It just is. I don't need to be defensive, because I respect myself as well and respond accordingly; I'm free to like it or not. I don't have to struggle. (Weird – I still expect to be burned at the stake every time I say I won't struggle.)

I have been coming back to a struggle with this quite often though, I admit, during a deep scrutiny of my identifying process. Do I just leave, as an answer to things I don't want, because I have identified with that reaction? Is that an image I have made for myself, which keeps me limited? Some desperado riding off into the sunset? "This is who I am, I leave for new places and ride horses – if I don't leave or don't ride, then I'm not being me." Have I put into a box what being true to myself is always going to be? Am I afraid I'm not being true to myself if I'm not being that? Am I just running from a fear that fear is running me? Good questions to ask, but do I need to assume my feelings are mistaken, incorrect, based in fear? Why not assume love is running me? Once again – moment to moment with no conclusions.

If I am surrendered to love and freedom, I just need to be in touch with my feelings and respond accordingly to the doors that open for me. **The key is to be truly in touch with my feelings – and that's the trick.** But if I choose to love my feelings, it's easier. To love them I just need to see them for what they are without having to say what they **should** be, or what they mean; then I'm in touch with what they actually are. And I don't have to knock on doors I don't like the feel of.

Maybe no door will open out of here, but I will feel what I feel anyway, rather than try to feel what goes with the apparent possibilities.

I write and talk like I get it but I still often slide back into the old pattern of trying to figure it out first, rather than feel it out. Second guessing my feelings, is basically to assume I'm delusional. But happiness is not dependent on enough of the right stuff (whether that stuff is time, money, or any other justifications). Happiness is our natural state. Unhappiness happens when we have conflict between what we are feeling, and what we are doing or trying to feel. That conflict only happens because we don't trust our feelings, or maybe don't even know what our true feelings are. It might be one of those times when we're being more concerned with whether or not "being happy with it" is settling for less, or maybe it's the old you-made-your-bed-so-you-have-to-sleep-in-it thing again. Fear of irrevocable mistakes.

The key is to be in touch with my feelings. (If I need a hint – what feelings would I like to give to my character if I were writing a story?) There's a lot of me that still doesn't believe my feelings are the only real thing to go on. That just seems too radical, and yet I can see that's where I'm headed.

Well that's my journal so far, for what it's worth. You'll notice some thoughts that reflect our past conversations. You make a good sounding board. Now I'm re-reading what you and U. wrote about selfishness. I think it also has to do with the subject of cricket watching.

I wonder about the origins of the word selfish. Did it ever mean the ish of self? You know, like the ish of green means greenish? Maybe in the past, somebody tried to help the victims by using guilt trips to make the perps afraid of judgment. The concept of selfishness as a totally unacceptable behaviour has certainly been effective as a tool of manipulation and control. And it certainly gets in the way of intuition as well.

I agree, we can't do anything that is not actually self oriented. I may choose to do kind and thoughtful things for others, things that are inconvenient, painful, or costly; but **I choose** to be that way – my self desires to be that. It's about self. If it's not, then it's not genuine, is it? It's not **heartfelt**. Instead it would be about approval and acknowledgements of selfless acts of generosity. Possibly for the purpose of building a debt of gratitude and obligation? Or privately, for the psychological security and satisfaction of knowing we're not that bad selfish thing? Ultimately it's about self, one way or another. (As U. says, no true friend would threaten you with promises of unselfish love.)

Maybe a new word or two would help. I could say, "I am going to cricketableishnessly go for a walk in the woods rather than do the bottle drive". And you could reply with, "That's very ipsissumus of you."

Looking forward to hearing from you.

Dear O.

Thanks for letting me share that with U. It got an interesting response. What do you think of this?

Daydreaming

We've heard that creative power is in the silent space between thoughts. Is that just another way to say "awareness"? Creative power is in awareness? I think so, in the sense that it is awareness that creates the space. Of course, I don't actually know much about the space (a silence that is between thoughts, naturally can have no thoughts in it) but it helps me to ponder on it this way.

I have patterns of thought that create my reality, consciously or otherwise. When I notice my thoughts and realize that I don't want to be creating anything of that vibration, there is an opening to new possibilities – a gap, a space between thoughts. It's like the awareness – Hey, I don't want that! What's going on here? – interrupts the pattern of thought. I can insert a new pattern into that gap in that instant before the old pattern has time to recover from the shock of awareness. In fact I can consciously build this new pattern and let it sit on the surface, in position. It will naturally fall into any available space, and leak through any cracks my awareness creates, no matter how small. All I have to do is be aware of what my thought patterns are – not that it's easy, but that's all. The rest will take care of itself naturally. Be aware, plus a little daydreaming won't hurt. Dream up the new pattern.

Yes, daydreaming. Or, here's a bigger word – psychocybernetisizing. (You know, cybernetics – the study of automatic control systems. And, no I didn't make up the word myself.) Some might prefer to meditate, and I suppose this may be just another form of meditation, but often I'd rather approach it as a daydream; it seems like more fun. For example, when I catch myself thinking people are idiots and a danger to my health, it presents a subject to daydream about, a new pattern to build. I can imagine beautiful, kind people everywhere, intelligent and thoughtful, smiling, helpful, laughing people all jubilantly wallowing in each other's success. (My mind of course will jump in with, "That's stupid, don't delude yourself, besides, you're wasting your time and you have more important things to do. What could all that bliss get you anyway?" It's just doing its job I suppose, but I tell it to take a break.)

I imagine detail, the more detail the better, because it gets to the feeling of it that way. Or maybe I could use the word emotion here. The creative power in anything you say, do or think is in the emotion, the passion. So imagine whatever gets you to the emotion you feel you want.

If I peel away the idiot skin off that dye haired politically incorrect youth over there for instance, I can imagine him noticing that little old lady struggling with the door. He runs over and with a great chivalrous flair, opens the door for his lady. This grumpy old woman straightens up and smiles, yes that face can smile! She doesn't assume he's going to mug her, she curtsies and nods to him as she graciously glides through the door he holds for her. It doesn't matter that this is not what-is in this moment. I don't need it to be. It's just practice, it's building new thought patterns, new vibrations.

I don't have to know that the water in the river is good to drink and play in before I think about it that way. I don't have to know that my bank account is large before I daydream my way to a sense of wealth. It can just sit on the surface till it falls into space; into the space my awareness creates.

If I want the best, why think the worst? I might see and smell dead fish floating on the river, and I may have a bank statement in my hand… but I can still imagine things how I want them, without being in denial of what is. I don't have to jump in for a swim or buy a new car to prove anything; I don't have to believe it. I can think of things the way they are in the picture I like best, instead of how they are in the picture I like least. Choose the vibes you like.

Sometimes when I have done this, I suddenly noticed something wonderful I had been overlooking. And then I would say, "Oh well that was there all the time, I just hadn't noticed it yet. It didn't really make a difference to think differently." But whether it was there all the time or not is beside the point; either way, I couldn't see it before. It seems that we see according to what we think. We can only see what has a compatible vibration with our thoughts.

I like the distinction O. made between feeling and emotion; it helps to convey thoughts on the subject with more accuracy. My thoughts are similar I believe: Feeling just is, with no reason, and it tells us what is in Accord. Emotion is energy motion; emotions move creative energy, and we can affect our emotions by use of imagination because emotions are all about reason. Pardon me for expounding, but I like this one: imagine whatever gets you to the emotion you feel you want.

~o~

I can daydream what ever pleases me, follow my happiness. It may seem easy in a way to just allow my imaginings to go where they will, but that is not necessarily following my happiness; it may just be following my old patterns. I can make the effort to notice how I feel though, and if I don't like how I'm feeling in those thoughts, I can drop them. In some areas I will just start with noticing that I **have** thoughts, and how they feel. I don't have to make them stop, or change them; awareness will do it all. I'll get out of the way and let it. Resistance and struggling just gets in the way, makes a depression, muddies the waters. Whenever the effort is fun and not a struggle (inspired, in other words) I will practice new patterns.

~o~

Today I noticed the thoughts that I don't **want** this to be a "rose garden" for me; I don't want to be happy here, I want to see "shit" because (or so I apparently believe) seeing "roses" would mean this is who I am. And that is disturbing I suppose, because it doesn't fit the image I have identified with. (Very tough to suspend beliefs about who I am.) There's also, "Loving and leaving means you're bad." I'm not sure where I came by those beliefs, but they both point to being miserable and unloving as the answer. (Good – more material for awareness to work with.) This is another example of how it **is** what we look at, not so much that we look at what it is. "Looking" all of sudden seems to be neither passive observation, nor a search.

What strikes me is that I'm refusing happiness when I come across it, because I am stuck on my ideas of where to find it. Why would I pursue happiness only by certain paths? Is it only happiness if I chase it down and tame it, ambush it at certain points on particular trails? If it comes to me and nuzzles my elbow, will I just slap it away as though it's worthless since I didn't control it and it's not following the rules? I think happiness is wherever it happens. I don't need to be miserable first in order to justify action that hopefully will eventually make me happy. Why go for the wild goose chase? Why not go straight for the happiness?

Now I get what U. said about choosing to be miserable for a good reason rather than being happy for no reason. It is actually a choice. I just needed to choose to be willing to look from a new perspective. I knew that, but it always surprises me when I find a new way to apply it.

Who knows, I might stay here forever. But I don't have to stay just because I love it, or leave because I don't have good enough reasons to stay. It's not love just if conditions are met. Love just is.

www.ingramcontent.com/pod-product-compliance
Ingram Content Group UK Ltd.
Pitfield, Milton Keynes, MK11 3LW, UK
UKHW020135250726
13967UKWH00002B/665